Once upon a Neighborhood

Once upon a Neighborhood

Evelyn D. Klein

North Star Press of St. Cloud, Inc.

Saint Cloud, Minnesota

Copyright © 2009 by Evelyn D. Klein.

All rights reserved.

ISBN: 0-87839-345-5
ISBN 13: 978-0-87839-

Library of Congress Control Number: 2009936284

Printed in the United States of America

First edition: September 2009

Published in the United States of America by
North Star Press of St. Cloud, Inc.
PO Box 451
Saint Cloud, Minnesota 56302
www.northstarpress.com

For my children,

Angie and Bill

ACKNOWLEDGMENTS

For their kind support in the final stage of the manuscript, a special thank you goes to Dr. Margaret Odegard for editing and to my son, Bill Bader, for technical help. Thank you, also, to North Star Press for their helpful suggestions about the cover.

Grateful acknowledgment is made to editors and publishers of journals and anthologies in which the following poems were first published:

Guild Press: *Full Circle 13*, "The Gift;" *Full Circle 14*, "The Season's Last," "Sumac;" *Full Circle 16*, "Visitor from Russia," "The Sound of his Voice."
Gypsy Cab: "Fabric of Continuity."
Midwest Chaparral: "Company," "The Cormorant," "Evolution," "St. Paul Dream 1992," "Looking Forward," "One Month Worth of Rain in Twenty-Four Hours," "Tribute to Richard Gisselquist."
Moccasin: "All Things New and Beautiful," "At Her Door," "Azalea," "Battle Creek Lake," "Black Canvas Shoes," "Invitation," "Monday Morning," "Omen," "The Pebble," "Viewing the Sun through Configurations," "At the Arboretum," "The Sound of His Voice, "Transplanting," "View," "Bill," "At Her Door, " Dancing Partner."
Northfield Magazine: "Demeter's Other Side."
Saint Paul Almanac: 2007, "A Taste of Minnesota, " 2008, Battle Creek Crossing."
Sidewalks: "Goodwill Bag."
Stage Two: *Poetic Lives:* "The River," "Shoes Any Color."

Table of Contents

Introduction ix
Free Spirit xi

I. In the Park

Reflections 3
Looking Forward 5
Battle Creek Crossing 8
The Pebble 8
Black Canvas Shoes 9
Sumac 11
Battle Creek Lake 12
Transition 13
World Without End 14
Demeter's Other Side 5

II. From My Window

Renewal 19
Atoms of the City 21
Azalea 23
Goodwill Bag 24
Breaking May Silence 26
The Gift 27
The Finches 28
One Month Worth of Rain in Twenty-Four Hours 29
Bill 30
Checking In 31
The Seedling Oak 33

Grace 35
Shoes Any Color 37
Viewing the Sun through Configurations 39
Evolution 40
The Season's Last 41
The Sound of His Voice 42
All Things New and Beautiful 43
Miss Minnesota 44
Act of Kindness 45
Fabric of Continuity 46

III. Neighborhood

Return 51
Omen 53
Downstairs Apartment 54
At the End of the Street 56
Last Day in April 59
Transplanting 61
Gathering 62
Three Women 65
Margaret 66
Friendly Encounters 68
Exhibition 69
Preparing the Move 71
Faces of Seasons 73
Bertha's Passing 75
Through Open Doors 76
Maynard 78
Laundry Room Turns 79
The Contest 82
Visitor from Russia 83

Before Christmas 85
Celebration 87

IV. Seasons of the Mississippi

River 91
The Journey 93
January 94
Saint Paul Dream 1992 95
Spring Eclipse 96
View 98
The River 99
Runaway 101
Spirits of Saint Paul 102
Monday Morning 104
Unfinished Train Ride 105
Mississippi River Excursion 107
Echoes of an Ordinary Day 109
At the Mississippi South of Saint Paul 112
Railroads 114

V. Around the Corner

Roads Between Cities 119
At Her Door 122
Como Park 123
Construction Zone 125
Wheels of Fortune 127
Starting Out 129
At the Arboretum 131
A Taste of Minnesota 132

The Man with the Rose 134
Company 135
First and Third Saturdays 136
Tribute to Richard Gisselquist 138
Chance Meeting 140
Balloon Extravaganza at the Dance Shoppe 141
Dance Partner 143
Twin City Valentine 144
At Saint Paul City Hall 145
Ice Palace Legend 147
At the Grocery Store 148
What's for Dinner? 149
The Spectator 151
The Field Across the Street 153
As the Blue Heron Flies 155
In the Dark 156

The Author 157

Introduction

Community. It keeps on changing, right along with our lives, people moving in and out, leaving primarily the framework. Does it still exist? Often community no longer denotes just the specific residential or political locale in which we live. It can draw much larger circles around the place of our residence. Most of us no longer live our entire lives in the community where we grew up. It frequently begins when families disperse, spread out, once the children grow up, as was the case in my family. Not only do we leave our parental home, but we may leave the area as well, move to another state or even to another part of the globe. Perhaps we even grew up in different areas, states, or even countries. That is the reality of twenty-first century America. The reasons for relocation may be many and as varied as the people. We may relocate to make a living, find a more agreeable climate, freedom of expression, for instance. Or we may relocate because of marriage, schools, war, homelessness, scenic beauty, and on and on. Of course, technology has made transportation and communication easy. And while it has made moving away easier, it also has brought us together, not only with new people but it has let us communicate more easily with those at a distance. Perhaps we communicate more in-depth when we are at a distance. Perhaps we spend the time together visiting with more compelling activities than we would have in a more casual setting of living in close proximity to each other. Some relationships may even thrive or reinvent themselves in this new exchange.

But when we leave the comfort and security of the parental home and the community in which we grew up or at least resided for an extended period of time, we tend to look for new connections. Whether we realize it or not, to fill our needs, we try to recreate the old or find a new community which so many of us crave when our other important relationships and familiar places are located in another part of the country. But whether we are new to a given area or we want to expand our present community, we may choose to do so on the job, at school or church, in organizations that we join, on daily errands, at a cabin or resort we frequent, etc., and, very often, with our new neighbors. This means we are not limited to any particular locale. And since this mix of people who were born in a given area and those that have moved in over the years is a common American phenomenon, just like the athletes that are recruited all over the United States for sports teams representing a given state, so the people who live in a given area represent the area. It, thus, becomes incidental as to who arrived there first as long as each resident contributes to the functioning of the community.

Once Upon a Neighborhood builds on the interactions of a diverse people who come together to form a community in the modern sense. Set against the backdrop of scenic beauty with the Mississippi River, parks and its many lakes, the community builds on its history, traditions and activities, not afraid to take the lead with progressive ideas and changes. Living in and contributing to this community fosters a sense of identity and belonging that carries the distinguishing mark of the Twin Cities of Saint Paul and Minneapolis.

Free Spirit

    When you live on your own
the world is
neighborhood and family
little by little you discover
who the people are
the way they talk and listen
the way the corners of the mouth
turn up when they smile

    the woman across the street
consults about house matters
the mechanic talks cars
the clerk is another mother
with whom to share
people at work are support team
and church is a way station
friends are family
and children home from college
are best friends

    home is the castle
where plants are children
God is parent
and parents are roots and direction
life is at a whim
to garden or go dancing
be home late for dinner
when you're sick it's time for a crash diet
there is always enough hot water
and no one lays claim to the TV
and when you hurry home with good news
you wonder why
you did not stay out late
to celebrate

1
In the Park

Reflections

The little park has become my place of reflection, as if to stop the clock as life turns the corner. Neither nature nor development remained the same in this old familiar park that now only bears resemblance to the way I first knew it. It has come of age with picnic areas, pavilion, playground, and water park in this landscape of change. The Park invites to linger. I remember past in light of present and look for paths into the future.

One side of Battle Creek Park still borders the woods near the development of homes to the east, where a ballpark has been added. Its meadow faces apartment buildings and town homes across, on the west side of the street. Battle Creek runs through the woods along the northern border of the neighborhood, feeding into the lagoon in the park. When we first lived in this area, my husband and I took the children for a hike once along the creek that ran past our back yard, exploring its course. Today I try to retrace the walk, starting out in the park, working my way backwards toward the neighborhood, over fallen trees and through thick underbrush. But the brush becomes too dense and tangled for me to make it back to the old back yard. No longer sure where I am, I stop just in time to see an egret rise above me. And I feel well rewarded.

In the past, the undeveloped park had a somewhat sketchy presence in my mind, consisting partially of woods and meadow where the lagoon stretched out. Since it had no picnic areas, it was not frequented as much by families as it is today. When the children were small, my parents came to visit, and my dad, who loved the woods, would take the children on walks to the park following the path from the street. They always brought back a story. Sometimes, when my children played outside, they occasionally slipped away. When they did not respond to my calls, I began to look for them, and directed by other children, I found them in the park, where they had discovered a new world.

"The little park," has now expanded south, across the street on Upper Afton Road, absorbing the area that once was part of the old Jordan farm. A modern single family home marked the farm's border along the street then. We sometimes went on hayrides through the woods with our neighbors and enjoyed refreshments at each other's homes afterwards. But the city had plans for the land. For a while, during Governor Wendell Anderson's tenure, this part of Jordan farm was considered as site for a new Minnesota zoo, while we all hoped it wouldn't happen. The house was eventually hoisted onto a frame and moved to a new location. Now this section of the farm has become the wooded extension of Battle Creek Park with paved biking and hiking paths, while the new zoo found a home in Apple Valley.

It feels good to breathe the fresh air of the park, be part of nature, watch birds – and people, who have become increasingly multicultural over the years. Sometimes, I have company. When my parents visited from Milwaukee, I wanted to show them around. But the walk proved too much for them, and they rested on the bench along the path instead. Most of the time, I come alone to this haven of community, my backyard of transition, often returning home with a poem rising above the sunset.

Looking Forward

Indian summer calls me
like a lover
to the park

    summer's last breath
    finds people feeding geese
    at the pond
    dark silhouettes
    against purple
    twilight canvas

    sea gulls circle
    one more time

    flocks of geese
    light from water

    they all follow the sun

Behind me the pond
lies empty and pale now
under a half moon
trees still burning
rust and gold

where I meet the sun
in the morning

Battle Creek Crossing

Two children follow their father
on bicycles
cross the street
to Battle Creek Park
single file
to the path
past dandelion meadow
whose rain-drenched scent
stretches along pregnant pond
and curves through the park

    Ducklings follow their mother
    on the pond
    she scrambles to shore
    little ones squirming
    up the small steep bank
    to rest hidden in grass

Song of red-winged blackbird
chirp of crickets
occasional duck calls
cries of children at play
harmony muffled momentarily
as a jet passes above
all are mine for the instant

    Reflections
    of past summers
    with my own two small children
    ripple on the pond
    in life's continuous flow

Spring has a different face
this year
now too sultry
then too cold
always the Minnesota lure
winter changed the trees
and us
we cross to the other side
pull life behind
till it overtakes us

The Pebble

on the path

   jumps

a penny-sized toad

makes me

   jump

laugh at myself

   glad

not having stepped

   on it

Black Canvas Shoes

Black canvas shoes
left at the path
in the park
point to the meadow
at dusk

small feet
having freed themselves
to trace time
across moist grass
to make cartwheels
childhood's infinite circles

sucking sweet clover
she looked at the ants
walking their trail
avoided quarrelsome geese
resting in evening sun

chewing a blade of grass
she watched mother duck
and long line of ducklings
at the pond

the girl twirls
around her finger
end of a pigtail
that will loosen
soon enough
into the flowing hair
of a woman

today life's newness
fills with wonder
beginning a story
in dreams
not yet turned wishes

until hunger
calls home

Sumac

      is
burning
    on the green knoll
passion
    of summer
spent

Battle Creek Lake

Driftwood
on September's slate green lake
comes to life
geese and ducks

they nestle in fall's
secret ritual

their somber domain
attended by night's
fading shadows

draped in veils of mist
as if guarded
by summer's ascending spirit

inside the fringe of trees
that holds back
the sun's eastern fire

Transition

Fall winds cross the land
brisk and cold
warmth of summer
a lover's half-forgotten memory

geese fill the air
in upbeat bands of sound and motion
settling on this Minnesota Lake
in peaceful reassembly

fall does not hold back
like someone afraid to speak
or a lover not wanting
to get in too deep

fall winds scatter golden leaves
across meadow to pumpkin patch
past burning bush
to wall of corn field

fall moves forward
now mild and sunny
then cold and harsh
roses and geraniums still blooming

fall on the way to meet winter
is predictable and steadfast
like geese flying south
and corn losing ground to houses

So when fall winds begin to blow
bring out the down coat
Lean into the winds
without looking back
Walk with them
into the next season

World Without End

Every afternoon
the elderly Hmong couple
cross the street
dodging traffic
to the park

They walk silently
except
for a brief exchange
now and then
he one step ahead
as if leading the way
to an unfamiliar adventure

They walk at a good pace
their grown children
having left them behind
tending their own children
advancing in the workday world
as they seek to master
the language of a new life

Going to the park
the elderly couple return
to the garden of being
where the language is universal
and they feel at home
in the scheme of creation

Every afternoon
the elderly couple
cross the street
to the park
until the snow flies

Demeter's Other Side

Halloween's surprise
casts a white winter mask
over Minnesota's
Indian summer days
replacing jack-o-'lanterns
with Christmas ornaments
in stores

       transforming Battle Creek Park
       into a wilderness of snow
       where on yesterday's summer meadow
       people lingered
       where on the olive-colored pond
       ducks fished
       in shadow of geese
       where red-winged blackbirds perched
       on reeds nearby
       and sea gulls filled the air

The snowy blanket now claims
the leg to the knee
footing is unsure
and wind gusts sweep hard
curling snow like smoke
across the park
threaten to down the visitor
into the snowy bed

       summer's paths have vanished
       and with them hikers and lovers
       runners and families
       children at play
       scent of picnics and roasts

I cannot make it to the pond
that bleeds dark brown
into the snow scape
where barely discernible
bird forms rise like spirits
in haze and dim light

turning around
I lean into the force of wind
that takes my breath and whips

ice needles into my face
I trace back my boot steps
painstakingly toe to heel
as if retreating
from a forbidden island

II
From My Window

Renewal

When we first lived in the area, we could see the blue 3M sign on top of the 3M Center building from the bedroom window of our old house. Like big brother, my husband's employer seemed to look down on us, radiating influence into our lives. Yet at the opposite end of the house, the living room window filled with African violets, opened our view down the street of a young family's beginning.

From my apartment window, I now can see 3M buildings and traffic rush past on I-94 in an endless stream, like life moving on. I still recall the widening of highway 12 into I-94 between I-494 and the St. Croix River in the late twentieth century. It brought with it, first, resistance to change, then, environmental controversy, ending in upheavals of earth. Eventually, the paradox of people moving further and further east in search of green space resulted in attention shifting to the increasing congestion that followed.

Roads I travel as a result of change connecting stages of my life are not always so obvious, as I am involved in life's tasks. After change has already occurred, it is often easier to assess where I have been and what led me to the new place. But the road ahead always seems obscure, no matter how well planned. Sometimes a detour brings me to some unfamiliar place. Sometimes I need to look for directions; at other times, I just forge ahead using the compass of intuition. Time has changed not only the landscape of my environment but the perspective of my vision as well.

I-94 past 3M Center was undergoing widening again in the twenty-first century but this time without controversy. In the meantime, homes, businesses, and roads have filled open spaces. A corn field next to a development now looks strangely out of place, just as an occasional house next to an open field once did. Every time I seem to have settled down to a comfortable pace, things change again with new buildings, street signs and roads moved or disappeared in the never-ending Minnesota building boom.

Like me, many of my former neighbors have moved on, too. From the street where I now live I can see Saint Paul's skyline that always raises my spirits as I approach on the freeway. Sometimes I wish I could stop the car right there to take a picture or do a sketch. From the lookout at Indian Mounds Park the skyline takes in the view in one breath – downtown, airport, river, bridges, railroads, roads – connecting past, present and future with Indian mounds and cathedral, capitol and skyscrapers, and transportation by land, air, or water, in this confluence of life's destinations, real and imagined.

The heart of Saint Paul, too, has renewed itself over the years, holding on to just enough landmarks like the public library, Landmark Center, and a few churches. By day, you find the people in government or new commercial buildings and on the street. You find them shopping during lunch hour in little shops in the skyways or at Macy's, formerly Marshall Field's that once was Dayton's, the only department store left downtown after the exodus of shops and stores to the suburbs. At night the city radiates peace with old-time street lights and lighted trees in parks. You wonder where the people are, then, unless an event at Xcel Energy Center, Ordway, Fitzgerald or another public event brings them out.

It is hard to know where one community ends, another starts, suburbs having attached themselves to the city's apron, like children to their mother. Thus, the community is no longer just where the family lives, works, shops but wherever people gather to share commonalities and diversities, where I can be who I am, without having to settle – a place where I feel I belong.

Atoms of the City

Like a benevolent spirit,
the moon casts its halo
above shredded clouds
and Saturday traffic,
lifts the tall 3M building
above city lights
and roads
out of flatlands
into the sky,
forming a pyramid—
granting night its third dimension.

Below, seeking its mark, energy
diffuses in four directions.
A roadway truck,
giant among midgets,
pulls ahead in the race,
while cars maneuver
nervously around it.
Passenger cars
and holiday inn vans
filter through the city
like atoms,
split direction somewhere,
disappear
behind an abutment,
a curve,
a building.
Hundreds of vehicles per hour,
carry humanity –
faceless, nameless, regardless
of race, creed, color, or national origin –
to obscure destinations.

A jet flashes past,
prepares to land,
in its belly
yet another metropolis,
ready to transfuse the city
which never sleeps.

Azalea

Life has become
   like the azalea
at Easter
   holding hope
in its buds

which now open
   petal by pink petal
revealing layers
   like reminders
of past springs

stems fan out
   lighting the room
with blossoms
   and the future
with new growth

Goodwill Bag

March sun casts long shadows
snowy brightness fills the room
drives violets to flower
and me to make room for spring
Ash Wednesday almost here
the closet offers nothing that inspires
only memories that no longer fit

from days when I made everything
clothes too hard to part with
await their fate like refugees
the polka dot sun dress
with the little jacket took me
through the French Quarter
in the spring of our marriage
unlike the see-through blouse
that wasn't me and still isn't
but the heavy wool suit
that brought highlights
to the ash in my hair
challenged my creativity like
the big house we built in the woods
heavy beamed ceiling and spindles
woodwork stained walnut
a house so big and dark you could
get lost in it and never know
the sun was out and the three-inch
brown heels I only wore when I had him
to hang on to for balance
in the winter of our season
browns and blacks and grays loom
a distant dream unwilling to fade

quickly I slip them into
the big plastic bag that
will trail others gone before
filled with the children's old things
baby clothes made room for toddlers clothes
and then for Cub Scouts and Brownies
and growth spurts like whirlwinds
brought them to band and choir as if
life were measured by clothes
while we lived vicariously with them

but I retrieve the blue-grey suit
for the color of my eyes
the rest to be recycled to make
someone else's life new and
satisfy my craving for fresh colors
memories turned tax deductions
shadows brought to light
a bag released to the world

Breaking May Silence

In the season
scented with lilacs
and cut grass
new beginnings
revisit thoughts
of old friends

two finches appear
on the patio's
rod iron railing
like a gift from above

vibrating with intensity
the male's
raspberry dipped head
stretches
toward the mate
he delivers his song
in repeated strophes

she faces him
motionless
as if absorbing
every note into
the roundness of her
earthen-colored form

he flies off
to the fringe of trees
and she follows
with that invisible bond
their fruitful connection

The Gift

Yellow marigolds
wait at home
    like children
I slip out of
the automated day
to let the skin breathe

    On the balcony
I transplant
sun-puffed blossoms
from crowded nursery pots
into planters

Here time is measured
with begonias unfolding
    rose petal-like blossoms
and progress
with impatiens driving
    pea-shaped buds
to flowering bells
and open faces

Outside my window
candle hours
light blossoms
that scatter petals on the floor
    of a new season
until leaves yellow

in this cosmos
I am the rain
that merges with the sun

The Finches

        Inside patio doors
        I pot African violets

outside the finch
watches me from her nest
in the hanging basket
of red geraniums

because motherhood
cannot be left to chance
with traffic in the street
and sparrows nearby

every day
she grows more reluctant
to leave her post

she is less afraid
for herself than
for her yet-to-be chicks

the mate never far away
warbles message or warning
from the trees

sometimes he visits
perches on basket wires
as if posing for pictures
but to see for himself
to make sure
because it takes two

        the mother finch watches me approach
        watering can in hand
        she moves over among leaves
        but this time
        she does not fly away

One Month Worth of Rain in Twenty-Four Hours

Outside my window
    flat garage roofs
undulate rain pelted
    like ponds

Rain having stopped
    two crows drop to bathe
and take off again
    a lone mallard wades
bobbing awkwardly
    trying to swim
in water too shallow
    protesting
he flies toward the park

    the building across
mirrors on the roofs
    the blurred image
of a dream
    on the invisible bridge
next to it
    shadows of traffic
move east
    released of the pent-up day

commuters take with them
    shadows of dreams
storm clouds hold down
    so they don't disappear
from the driver's view

    people rush home
extinguish the shadows
    and fall back into step
of every night

    I am grateful
the storm kept me inside today

Bill

    After he had left
    for college

I came up the ramp
from the weekly grocery trip
when an old Dodge charger
rushed across the overpass
before me

    I strained to recognize
    the tall dark figure

waving at me through
dark tinted windows
of an unfamiliar world
he passed and I followed

    in our driveway
    my son emerged

from his newest vintage car
ready to take its turn
in the driveway
like the models on his book shelf

    getting out he smiled
    and stood much taller
    than I remembered

Checking In

    She arrives
    like the robin in spring

I look up at
her half-moon smile
that reflects the sunshine
of green eyes in a frame
of strawberry blond hair

ready to embrace
the unexpected and me
her mother
she sings rapid strophes
of friends and days' events
with refrains of
"It's good to see you"
accented by intermittent hugs

    After she learned to walk
    she explored the house
    discovered cupboards and toys
    treasures she examined
    or loaded onto her toy wagon

    at intervals she dashed out
    as if rediscovering
    wrapped arms around my legs
    precariously in action
    our eyes met and she drank
    the milk of our connection
    squeaking contentedly then
    she tossed golden curls
    padded off to disappear behind
    the door of a new adventure
    until time to refill again

Now we both recline and lounge
in our talks where we inhabit
common space in our garden of genes
having grown through childhood together

discussing psychology class
we push out fences
she takes a first run
I a second
at the shadow and the mountain

      Cutting the cord
      for the thousandth time
      she flies off like the robin
      after its evening song
      until the next time she drops in

The Seedling Oak

for Bill

    grows
        transplanted
from beneath shade
of old scrubby white oaks
whose knotted limbs
stretch leafless
here and there

    shock fades
into new growth
as roots grasp hold
    nourished
by fresh earth and
open space
    it reaches
toward sun and rain

    expands
to full potential
despite seasonal storms
    grows past brush
prickly ash
and maple

    the white oak
does not snap
like the aspen
    holds its ground whole
more and more
    each season

the only tree
to keep rust
of autumn leaves
through winter months
    creating wonder

    the white oak flourishes
more with each spring
    and soon lays claim
    to its own space

Grace

      We sit down at the table
with the hand embroidered
table cloth of a woman's pink
red and blue days
sun-colored centers
green future
in a tracing of steps

the minister among us
reverently asks His blessing
for the friendship
we are about to receive

      six or seven women gather
      weekly like for reunions
      we pass the meal
      move through the courses
      of this new age
      that finds childhood changed
      and aging parents in another world
      young parents in the middle
      the workplace beckons
      with promise and escape
      yesterday's struggle
      becomes today's nostalgia
      we drink the water
      of common experience and
      share the bread of newly found ways
      photograph the moment
      until laughter tops dessert

we close the window on noise
of traffic and mower that threaten
to drone out women's voices

once more we examine hand stitched hem
of an existence that connects us

this gift
the making of meals
we pass it along
each according to our chosen design

Shoes Any Color

In front of the bookshelf
next to my desk
shoes line up in a neat row
white and black
beige and black
sandals and pumps
heels and flats

Women's shoes are not made
for walking but to show off
the ankle and lengthen the leg
enhance the body
from behind and in front
the height of the heel
directly proportional to the
amount of beauty and discomfort
a woman can bear

In biblical times feet
were sometimes anointed
I wonder if Adam felt
Eve's legs needed help
why Lady Godiva let her hair
down when heels could lift her
why Chinese women had their
feet bound when
stilettos could free them

Placing myself at risk
of violating
the long-legged look
the height of my heels
decreases as

the number of shoes
increases in search
of the perfect pair
that will take me where
I want to go without
the wind blowing me over
crossing the street
to meet my date

Viewing the Sun through Configurations

Rocks and pyramids
dot the globe
in line with constellations
array of past civilizations

How long ago
this eternity

People numerous
as grains of sand

we trace footsteps
of parents before us
from one state to another
across cultures and continents

and overtake them
back into
the next eternity

Evolution

We cannot walk on
soil or sand
without leaving footprints
on concrete they echo
even if they have no name

and if the wave
of our presence sweeps us along
from farm country to
skyscraper city
and a greater distance
between delivery
and departure
it is not because
we are better
or smarter
but because of
the footsteps
bronzed for another age

in the end
we can fight the wave
and slip behind
or drown
or we can ride the crest
to the lap of the changing beach

The Season's Last

geranium blossoms
a pink and red cluster
        I gathered

the way I used to
when you were
on your way

placed it into a small
round-bellied vase
to save
        from frost

it lights up the table
like a promise
on the edge of the room
where we connect
        long distance

The unopened blossoms
soon reveal red tips
but then droop limp

while the bouquet's
        red petals
fall
   a circle
        around the vase

The Sound of His Voice

and fancy
wants to fly
to the stars

cast aside
last summer's
disappointments
and doubts

old hopes
cover grey landscape
with fresh snow

snow blindness
follows footprints
of past springs

into his presence
that sparkles
in snow crystals

holding promise
that melts again
with February snow

All Things New and Beautiful

December reluctant
to make room for winter
accompanies

mornings heavy
with darkness
rush hour gathers
light for the workday

evenings fall
before supper
fade into night
before we are home

gust suddenly scrambles
dry leaves
to some obscure spot
across the street

north wind blows in white
covers the diminishing year
displaces fog's chill
hugs us close as we

propel forward into
light's forgetfulness
toward the warmth
of oncoming days

Miss Minnesota

In weekly meditation over a garden of violets,
I consider the pink African violet whose
rose petal-like blossoms extinguished
gradually, a friendship gone dry.

The blossomless leaves of this gift
having bloomed profusely for years, like
the friendship, die back on a wooden stem, curling
on soil's surface with only a few thread-like roots.

Bright January light invites to cut the stem
close to the plant, set the violet in water
of renewal that, under my watchful eye,
the friendship may draw new roots.

Once transplanted in fresh soil, Miss Minnesota
is sure to drive new blossoms, as I ponder anew,
how they cover lush new leaves,
in the process of regenerating the friendship

that wanted to move from plastic to stone
flower pot, to take center stage once more
in the line-up of African violets and friends
in the natural flow of things.

Act of Kindness

The shimmering violet-blue of lapis lazuli enchants
its veins connect to the exotic and to ancient times.

In the bathroom, I drop the brand new earring
that slides down the drain quicker than instinct.

When the plumber arrives at the quarantined sink,
I conclude: "You sound so New York."

With pained look, he reaches into cabinet to open drain.
"The woman on my last job asked me about my foreign accent."

I never thought of New York as a foreign country. He assured:
"But I was born in New York City and grew up there," his voice shaking.

I could have told him my niece works in New York City
or that I first arrived there a long time ago. Instead,

I recounted a visit from Minnesota to New York City, where I drove
through heavy traffic, while my husband buried himself in the map.

Two men in the car next to ours motioned to roll down the window.
The driver asked: "Where do you want to go?"

Their directions quickly took us to the United Nations building,
leaving the only things to watch out for those dented taxi cabs.

"The excitement of New York gets into your bones," I say,
"and the sound of the people lingers like a song."

The plumber's smile returns as arm retracts from drain.
"Here it is!" He holds lapis earring up against light and studies it.

He, then, hands me a bill for the minimum charge, and we part
like old friends, leaving me with the twice paid for gem.

Fabric of Continuity

Hands so used to write
now reach out to sew again
thread curls

    like grandmother's tendrils

I thread the needle

    grandmother's eyes probe
    with father's look
    from his drawing
    the actress's dream
    submerged in husband and children

with invisible stitches
I sew hem to slacks
the way mother might

    parts of two lives
    that need joining like
    mother marrying father
    to face raw edges
    of her childhood
    and his artistic zeal

I finish with silky lining

thread knots
I break it
start over

    after the dead end
    of our union

release the tension
ease material and stitches
on the slacks
try them on like a new life
as the children try theirs
I allow for movement and wear
the changing figure
the lower heel shoe stylish now
a woman's freedom
to move life forward

III
Neighborhood

Return

The east side of St. Paul used to be home for a time. Starting over in mid-life, I returned for a second look. After all, most of my friends still live here. How would I fit in after all this time? I used to rush past the old neighborhood on the way to St. Paul without paying much attention to how it changed, just as I did not pay much attention to how we changed. Children grow up, to be sure, but life simply seemed to go on as usual for the rest of us as we traveled new and widened roads. I now take stock, trace developments back. Reorienting myself to the old neighborhood is like reorienting myself to life itself. I recognize changes in the natural course of things in the family sphere and at work. Life has changed, as irrevocably in response to changes in the outside world as it has to those at home, having drawn us into its vortex.

The east side of St. Paul certainly filled out, replacing green areas with buildings and roads. The past seems but a blurred picture, the layout vaguely familiar but its face altered. The tall building with the red 3M sign, that used to be blue, still dominates 3M Center and surrounding neighborhoods. Looking for old landmarks, I find my way in new surroundings and begin to settle in among the changes. New access roads now lead to Sunray Shopping Center with new shops. At the east end, Cub Foods, a craft store, have replaced dime store. Fanny Farmer and post office moved already years ago, as I recall. At the west end, T.J. Maxx and other shops replace Wards Appliances and Minnesota Fabrics, where I used to spend hours planning sewing projects, while my toddlers danced to background music.

J.C. Penney and German import store are gone, too now. But, the drug store, relocated from east to west end, has expanded, upgraded, even added a drive-up window. By the time any of these changes occurred, we had moved long ago, moved east to expand and improve our lives and living space in line with expectations for the future.

Upper Afton Road has been improved past Battle Creek Park with an island in the middle of the road and a left turn lane into the park. At first I returned as if life could be shifted into reverse. But now I revisit to survey and reevaluate while I move life into the next stage whatever, wherever that may be. I find the old neighborhood still nestled hidden behind trees next to the park, extending between creek and road, north and south. I cannot resist seeking out the old house. Young boulevard trees that once let the eye move down the bright street in one glance have matured, and now fill out the space with their limbs and leaves, leaning over street like curtains, obscuring sky and homes. Sometimes we fill our lives to the point where we can no longer see what really matters. We go about our business matter-of-factly, until we come to a dead end. My eyes now strain to recognize, place former neighbors' houses, until they come to rest, at the end of the street, on the old house, our first home. Through dim haze of distance, it too, appears changed, a faded picture, rust colored roof tile replaced with charcoal tiles, the beige house light grey now, rust colored shutters replaced with dark grey ones at living room window. Few shrubs and no flowers decorate the yard. Lantern and planter are gone, too, like a life stage that has extinguished.

Still, it feels good to return to this place of happy times, where the children were little, and we lived the suburban life style, at last part of the community. The house remains landmark and testimonial to the way we lived then, measure of the distance we traveled, my way station from which to move forward, prerequisite of subsequent moves like sequels to a story.

Omen

Never before have I seen
sea gulls swarm and sweep quietly
low above my head like swallows
nearly brushing with their wings
the four-story apartment building
next to me

beneath feathered grey clouds
and patches of topaz
their movements seem conducted
as they stroke the domed sky
crisscross and in generous circles

among the multitude
one suddenly flutters as if
having struck a wrong note
another nearly flips as if
having missed a beat
but the one drops into flight
the other a glide
harmony restored

All that just before dusk
a melody by which to remember
a summery Friday in October

Downstairs Apartment

In the downstairs apartment
the young man lives alone.
His girl friend often visits, jumps over
porch railing, knocks on the glass door.
Two small boys fill the quiet
with their sounds on odd days and weekends.
Sometimes the grandmother sits with them
on the floor by the patio door,
like the good witch of Oz,
drinking coffee from a mug.
The boys like to explore
their father's red truck, under and over,
while he looks on from the patio.
They call out "Hi!" to passing residents
and hide their faces when asked their names.

Inside, father and children
often compress daily existence
into hours of radio scenes
frenzied laughter turning frantic tears
that ebb away worn.
Then only the steady hum
of little voices remains
so familiar and near
I feel transposed in time and space.

Last night I awoke to children crying.
I wanted to reach out in the darkness,
comfort and rock the babies
on a seesaw between two worlds.

A man's voice echoed,
"Shut up! Shut up!"

and leveled off a distant drone.
Then silence held the night again,
and I dropped back into the capsule
of my own existence.

At the End of the Street

        At the end of the street,
behind canopy of trees, the old house looks bare,
grey, all but disappears in the distance
like a faded, old snapshot.

The Austrian pine we had planted and pruned
has grown tall, straggly. Petunias and planter
with the lime stone border my father-in-law placed
during his visit from Germany are all gone –
gone like the young family who once lived there.

       This was our first house.
We found it in the snows of winter
and occupied it in the green of spring.

Decorated with sheer curtains and drapes,
the large living room became hub of activity,
its picture window lined with African violets,
where we could see up the street of expectations.

Here the children inhabited worlds of their own.
I often sat on the front stoop watching
my small children play in the yard. Sometimes
they brought friends to play in the breezeway.

These were times of our nightly ritual, when I,
sitting on the living sofa, one arm around each child,
read bedtime stories to them,
like *The Gingerbread Man, The Cat in the Hat*, and such,
until they were old enough to read them to me.

Their dad would sit in the rocking chair
across the room and chuckle over the stories,
as he and I grew up once more with our children.

Here is the backyard where, under the big willow,
I spread a blanket on the lawn for the toddlers
to welcome spring with a picnic.

In this house they learned to ride bikes, the girl
with training wheels and encouragement, the boy
with determination to catch up with the older sister.

When they started kindergarten, I had them pose
for first-day-of-school pictures each year. They
carried lunch pails with cartoon characters, and
returning home, they brought many stories to tell.

Grandparents came from Milwaukee to visit at Easter
each year and stayed in the downstairs bedroom,
the sewing room. They brought gifts like toys, cakes,
and clothes. Grandma taught the grandchildren
to count from one to ten in German. Grandpa
took them for long walks to Battle Creek Park.

     These were my stay-at-home-mom years,
when I learned to stretch income like children's socks
across the wash line, when I took sewing
and tailoring lessons to express my artistic side
in the family wardrobe, while helping to make ends meet.

At last, I made my driver's license to manage
while my husband was away on long business trips,
took courses at the U for relicensing, looking
back and forth over the fence of being.

In this neighborhood I learned to be neighbor
and member of the community at morning coffees
with the women, monthly card playing parties
with couples, and gifts for sick neighbors and charities.

The house at the end of the street,
behind canopy of years, stands with landscaped shrubs,
cream-colored siding, rust-colored roof and shutters,
red and white petunias around the lantern, a memory
etched a treasured picture of younger, simpler days.

Last Day in April

Coming out onto the landing
of the apartment building entrance
a woman and two girls
suddenly freeze
a motion picture
halted in track

>the woman's head
>of dark brown
>cascading curls
>never moves

>"I wanted to talk to you
>last night"
>the man says softly
>from the lawn
>light brown hair
>a wreath around his head

>the woman and girls
>descend the steps
>he the grassy hill alongside
>they walk to the car
>where she lets the girls in
>on the passenger side
>then unlocks
>the driver's side

>he keeps talking
>arms slightly raised
>palms open
>supplicant
>she closes the car door again

turns to him
buttoning her coat
slowly
as they talk
button
after button
after button

Transplanting

Last year
her potted tomato plants
starters of an independent life
climbed tall
up iron banister rods
heavily laden with fruit
that mocked
the north exposure

This year
the new neighbor
having planted seedlings
of a new season
sweeps soil spillings
off empty porch
with the energy
that marks borders
of newlywed promise

Gathering

Summer's geese flock to the pond
in the park
approaching people
      with handfuls of bread

Winter's people gather in the foyer
of recycled days
having stepped out of satellite news
      of Bosnia and Mideast
      political campaigns
      and crime in the Midwest

they await mail to bring them
bits of their world
      "He is late today" Don says
      shuffling in
      helping to fill the room
      with the leisure
      of those who have been there

the postman enters
from the snow scape
carrying unanswered wishes
      fills their expectations
      with new days

they cast rays of conversation
on the bench of their community
      Ron says Morley from downstairs
      went to Phoenix for the season
      Mary from upstairs
      went to a nursing home
      Ron will fix the coffee maker

        for the neighbor down the hall
        before she's off again
        to Canada this time
        Nancy will tend her flowers
        take in the mail

The young mother and the child
not yet used to her legs
enter the circle
        snow capped faces light up
        over their "adopted" child
        or grandchild whose smile
        and first steps count days
        their years in memories
        the girl stops
        near the woman with the cane
        on her daily walk
        tiny elbows hug tiny body
        freezing her smile in her tracks

        "We hope to move into our new home
        before Christmas" the mother says
        intercepting the little explorer
        at the door

Those coming home from jobs
slip into the dinner hour
        almost unnoticed and breeze
        through the foyer with drafts
        their greetings trail with them
        up stairs and into elevators

the postman's mailbox panel closing
scatters people who came
to connect
they collect their daily mail

"Just bills and advertisements
today" goes the refrain
as they all disperse

like the geese that clear the pond
with echoes of voices across fall days
making room
for the silence of winter

Three Women

Crowned
with salt and pepper curls
    they sit on back steps
    this afternoon
watch the Indy 500
of rush hour pass
on the freeway

    caretakers of the day
they welcome residents home
dispense weather reports
and forecasts
ready to expand conversation
    relate
recipes and news
of who moved in or out
or announce the president's
latest proposal

    in summer
their patios come alive
    with talk and laughter
mocking the fullness
of bygone family-filled days

    at night
    they shuffle the world
in their cards
as if they held
    both
    past and future
in their hands

Margaret

The virus invaded
his body and she
cared for him
as for a child

    food no longer
    pleased him
    until nothing did

She grew tired
too tired to remember
her weak heart

    her cheeks ebbed
    under red blush
    while she visited him
    in his hospital room

He was eager
to return home
she at a loss

    Not as she used to be
    when she saw him off
    to his retirement job
    when she stood
    at the building entrance
    Demeter at the gate
    chatting with neighbors
    as they passed by

"I love you"
she said
and he was gone

Soon after
waiting in her sister's car
in front of the grocery store
her shadow also rose

Friendly Encounters

Locking the apartment
he tends for a neighbor on vacation
the lithe figure
of a grey Prometheus
approaches briskly.
"Hello!" I say.
"Your potted tree
fell over again,"
he responds, hand on chin.
"I tied it with string,
but it broke in strong wind."
"Filament tape will hold it,"
he says.
"Perhaps the wind will stop…"
"Oh, but it won't. The tree
will fall over again," he says
as if in charge of securing trees
and single women.
"You must tie it well. I
can give you some tape."
"Thanks. I think I have some."

      And so on the patio
      of my new living space,
      I stand up the tree again
      like a troubled friend
      hoping for new growth
      to fill the void.
      I replace twice broken string
      with tape
      in renewal
      of life's expectations.

Exhibition

The year Republicans declared
"year of the woman,"

    my parents, already in their eighties,
came from Milwaukee to visit me in the apartment
of my new-found independence in Saint Paul
on occasion of Dad's art exhibit.

    On walk or errand, when Mom
accompanied Dad, they would walk
a harmonious unit, hand in hand or arm in arm,
Dad the leading spirit.

    As we leave for the exhibit,
Dad labors, with arthritic knees, to the door.
Mom abruptly slows down
and remains behind him half a step.

    "Well, are you coming?" he asks.
She speeds up, as if lost in thought,
then slows down again every time
she gains on him.

    On the street, he takes her hand.
"Oh yes," she says,
with her secretive smile and wink,
"that helps."

    The waterfall of Dad's
observations along the way
fills the well, the deep blue depths
of her eyes and soul.

Her still waters carry the ship
of his artistic creativity – and she
navigates the course of his life
which embraces her treasured world.

At the Republican National Convention,
no woman ran for high office that year.

Preparing the Move

Two crows call the dinner hour
from garage roofs

he drives the new red Neon
into Sunday peace
but not to take his turn washing it today

she brings out a large brown box
slides it with resolve into the back seat
while he holds open the door to their future

dark brown curls frame
her knitted brow
short blond hair
softens his smiling eyes

she carries a load each time
the young couple walk back and forth
together between patio and car
slim and even-shouldered
wind inflating their shirts like sails

she returns with another box
of accumulated months
then with garment bags and men's
shirts and ties on hangers
smoothens and straightens them
over the boxes as over a well-made bed
ready for a long journey

he looks on as pots fall
from her hands to the pavement
she squirrels the pots away

here and there inside the car
as if it were a nest

she watches while he returns
pregnant Neon to garage
their old grey Ford waiting empty
at the curb

   As the couple disappear behind patio doors
   sparrows reclaim their bush outside

Faces of Seasons

Sparrows scurry
for spilled seeds on the ground

    Rose was always around
    as sure as the lattice on the buildings

    on snowy winter days she'd bundle up
    and walk to the store
    on warm summer days she'd don swimsuit
    and follow the sun with lawn chair and paper

Rose attracted the sparrows
with her feeder
flocks perching on railings nearby

    on mild days her porch door stood open
    an invitation to fresh air and friends
    decorations of seasons always trimmed her doors
    she was in and out any weather with chores of sorts

    Rose colored the apartment complex
    with her sun tanned personality etched
    into the still-young face
    crowned white at seventy-two

she attracted the squirrel
that marked peanut shell trails across porches
connecting her world with the neighbors

    dispensing neighborhood news to passersby
    she once said in passing
    she'd miss the view if she moved

    but one day she vanished leaving
    bare apartment doors
    wind sweeping her porch
    gone to live with one of her children they say

She left behind the sparrows that now forage
on the ground in front of her patio

    until one day the curtain closes
    over her patio door
    behind a young couple just moved in

Bertha's Passing

A flurry of life
converges like pigeons
at the quiet apartment complex

    lung cancer
    had claimed her

children and grandchildren
great grandchildren
cross the lawn

    no one had ever
    seen them before

carrying African violets
ivy and spider plant they move
between buildings and cars

    single file like ants

filling the air
with unfamiliar voices
they leave a trail

    of cigarette butts

Through Open Doors

      In the hallway of transience
      the young mother approaches us
      child in arms

"Show how old you are"
      we watch a tiny hand uncurl

"No not five"
      the mother's big fingers
      separate tiny fingers

"You only wish you were five
so you can go to school"
      the mother says

            Just the year before young parents
            had returned from their honeymoon
            asking the sitter
            if the baby had missed them

"I'll take good care of her
till you get back from school"
      the neighbor says
      reaching for child and toys

"They've lived here for five years now"
      the neighbor says
"he'll start his new job up north soon
she and the baby will stay with her parents
until she finishes school"

"I like the little ones
they keep me company since Marv died"
      the neighbor adds with a laugh

Child in arms she disappears
behind the door
of her clean-scrubbed universe

I retreat across the hall
into the casual disarray
of my working life's domain

Maynard

Maynard rents his garage
to a neighbor
when he leaves before winter

he returns to Minnesota
with the robins
taps from garage to building
wearing white shoes
sports coat and casual pants
white flat top hat and a smile
Maurice Chevalier
of the Florida set

Sometimes he closes
the garage door
for the woman
who lives upstairs
and tells her
she drives much too fast

Laundry Room Turns

Across entry hall, the laundry room serves
a way station of observation and interchange.

Kitchen curtained windows
face the world home-like
in this public place, where people wait
on machines and try to recognize
between loads bits and pieces of lives
of people coming in or passing outside.

This is my place to sort past and fold present,
set future like hope into the basket of continuity.

>The retired woman down the hall
>claims the space around five o'clock daily.
>
>Armed with laundry caddy and book,
>she arrives. When both washers work,
>she drapes body and book over one washer,
>ignoring the chair in the corner.
>When it is time to change loads,
>she removes each piece of laundry,
>shaking it, then cracking it like a whip
>before folding, never turning her head.
>
>I wait, until she departs,
>laundry neatly draped over her cart.
>She responds with a silent smile to "Hello!"

The elderly woman from across the hall
moves her cart over when the second washer is free,

so we can catch up on life.
She turns down her radio,
and we discuss concerts
while she folds daisy sheets
just like the ones I once owned.
She tells of her camping trip
to the Boundary Waters
belying her age and petiteness of figure.
She scrutinizes each piece
she removes from the dryer,
making light over concern
for her son who is close to my age,
and I wonder
if parents will always be parents.

Finished, she leaves me
to the lone hum of machines
and the sound of traffic outside.

    The man from the other end of the hall
    takes up the washer just emptied,

    remarks on the balmy spring day,
    his eyes traveling between
    blouses hanging on wall rack and me
    as if to fit them for size.
    He leaves the room and soon returns
    to roll a colorful, fluffy ball
    out of dryer and into basket.
    He says he is expecting his children
    who visit weekly and studies the load
    I just removed from the dryer
    to ascertain once more my identity.
    I respond that my college-age children
    visit whenever they can.

>   Basket under one arm he leaves
>   in happy anticipation.

This ritual of washing clothes
as if to make life new again,

smoothing sheets like problems
of busy days and restless nights,
folding laundry as if to accept
that life begins anew each day
as pristine as the first snow
allows me to fit life neatly
into the basket of this new beginning,
with the sense that things, after all,
are well ordered, at least for tonight.

The Contest

    In the parking lot
two crows and two gulls
face each other
in a paved desert
    advance and retreat
time and again
    between them a plump
    hamburger doggie bag
gulls command the field

    A momentary stand-off

gulls advance again
    crows counter
they all swirl in a dance of combat
    crows stagger
    their shadows escape
into the air
    one gull rises

The remaining gull
leans into his gait
wings horizontal
    a triumphant general
    carrying battle plans
he charges his bounty
a watchful eye
on waves of traffic

    Above the hardware store
    two crows watch

Visitor from Russia

Across the table
the man from Russia
smiles
behind wire rimmed glasses

They search for common ground
for the right words
of a language
he has not yet mastered
being not yet transplanted like
the rest who blend in

yet his blond receding curls
and anvil hewn chin
fine tightly drawn lips
are like a mirror
of the German husband
except for the soft hands
that hold the water glass
pass the rolls

Not soldier or official
but healer
who brought a friend
from the old country
for treatment
he sits
against the graffiti
of past politics
in the company of two women
once rooted in German soil

They seek to know him
and his uncertain future
he is here doing odd jobs
awaiting his friend's healing
the quiet man from Russia
who speaks neither English
nor German
who eats vegetables and meat
at the American table
and whose name happens
to be Schulz

Before Christmas

The new father
carries the child
downstairs
on wings of a new age

he places her
in the mother's vehicle
with motor running
and leaves her there
while he gets the green truck
that usually hauls
nursery trees
he then transfers the child
and big bag into it
secures her
on the front seat of his day

the new mother
lightened of her charge
for now
scrapes ice of past tradition
off the red car's windshield

stepping close to him
by the truck door
she smiles
softness of dawn
while they talk

he kisses her
she steps back
as in a fertility dance
speaks to the movement

of a hand gesture
she kisses him

both get into their days
and drive off
until the circle of errands
brings them home again

Celebration

      for Bruni

We go to a movie
for change of pace,
the company, and the laughs.
Afterwards,
she invites me to her house,
since it is too early
to call it a night.

In the living room,
she builds a fire
against night's window,
lights a red candle
for life's neglected hours
and for the friendship.

She fills the room with Chopin,
the cups with decaf,
and we munch left-over "Stollen,"
discussing the usual topics,
the widening gap between rich and poor,
the mystery of men,
houses and the hostess' new furniture,
window on an artful Japanese garden.

We leaf through a montage
of remembered moments,
her parents in the old country,
where we stop only briefly,
as in a distant room.
We talk of jobs,
her garden parties and friends,

where languages, like tributaries,
flow into the American river
of the universal language
of people who live between two worlds
and find Van Dyke's Pieta,
Mozart's Magic Flute,
skyscrapers and remnants
of the Oregon Trail,
friendship and marriage
and children growing up
in unexpected ways
and much too soon.

The fireplace radiates
a fading rainbow.
And we hug good-bye
as the candle burns down
for the new times ahead.

Outside,
the spacious garden sleeps
beneath thick blankets of white,
waiting to fill the air
with scents of spring
and sounds of life.

The streets are hollow,
black now –
my tunnel to the stars.

IV
Seasons of the Mississippi

River

Almost everywhere you go in the Twin Cities, you run into the Mississippi River. It is like a spirit snaking its way through our lives, holding us in its spell. Roads, streets, and neighborhoods conform to its path. Boats and barges travel in its current like blood cells. Barges exchange cargo with railroads on its banks. Railroad yards and industrial complexes, large and small, whose chimneys send up smoke like banners, spread out on its flood plain. These alternate with other buildings, apartments, houses, and parks on the shoreline. Trees, bluffs and caves claim the remaining space. Outside Saint Paul, historic Fort Snelling along the shore, once clearly visible from a distance now sleepily nestles behind trees, a reminder of our changing presence. Modern bridges cross the river at regular intervals, bridges so large they seem to lift us into the sky. They dominate the landscape, like modern-day lookouts, where the magic of the river draws the eye no matter how we feel about bridges, sending imagination on never-ending journeys.

The Mississippi's face changes daily, with the weather, time of day, river traffic, always drawing my attention. If I do not scan or at least glance at it in passing, I have missed the activity, the mood, the fullness that rounds the daily experience. Crossing the river on the I-494 bridge into South Saint Paul on my way to work, it may greet me mysterious as misty mornings, reassuring as glowing sunsets, peaceful as a winter blanket of ice, oblivious as a veil of snow, threatening as a storm, bold as spring waters on a flood plain, distant as a shipping route.

It is hard to imagine headwaters of this River, seemingly a little more than a trickle, over which I jumped some years ago at Lake Itasca in northwestern Minnesota, gather into such a powerful force by the time it reaches the Twin Cities. Here the Mississippi drops over Saint Anthony Falls and is more than one thousand feet wide, joined along the way, in this area, by the Minnesota and Saint Croix Rivers.

  I like to stop and contemplate the Mississippi whenever and wherever I can, having grown up on Mark Twain's *Huckleberry Finn* and *Tom Sawyer* and then read to my students from *Life on the Mississippi*. I have become a sort of vagabond traveler, releasing myself into the river's spell, the confluence of daily reality and timeless imagination that works in different ways at each location and occasion, and let everything else drop away. Indian Mounds Park in Saint Paul is a good place to observe the river that demands full attention to sketch or pen – for it holds one thousand stories or more. When I travel Shepherd Road to Twin Cities International Airport or home from downtown Saint Paul, the river always makes me wonder what human stories reflect in current of its waters. Above, bluffs with Indian Mounds and Saint Paul's Cathedral beyond, the city in the background, Holman Field Airport, railroads, and *St. Paul Pioneer Press* newspaper on banks below, all stand sentinel to our advancement. From the distance, they draw a circle of communion between spirits of yesterday and today in a union, where I become one with my surroundings, transported with indivisible power on the collective journey to tomorrow.

The Journey

These words on paper
like anchored barges
on the river
are waiting
for the journey south

January

Bright with lights
    but without its load
the tugboat breaks out
    of winter's paralysis
like a first sign of spring
    eager to connect
impatient to renew
    traffic of life
on the mist-bedded Mississippi

And when geese
    string horizon
above tree lines
    flanking the river
then January thaw
    tempers Minnesota air
with longing

Saint Paul Dream 1992

On the windy Super Bowl Sunday, unexpectedly
cars back up on the freeway, rush-hour style.

In the distance, the ice castle, made of blocks
    hewn from the lake of wishes, glows ghostly
blue in a harbor of incandescent street lamps.
    Its walls release colored lights that explode
to music, drawing onlookers into translucent
    childhood dreams, where fairy godmothers watch
over children, and witches live in remote forests;
    where princes sleep all day long, and frogs
turn princesses; where swords have magic powers,
    and kings conduct just wars, somewhere
far away; where plagues won't fall from a burning
    sky; where benevolent despots help the poor
and ban offenders to the tower of no vision.
    There little girls are called to be lawyers,
engineers or cheerleaders and little boys
    to be football, hockey or movie stars;
there stars fall to earth gold coins;
    the prince slays the fire breathing dragon
to win the princess, and they live separately
    ever after in polarity of a debt-free kingdom.

February shadows recall uncounted spirits;
released into the river for the journey south,
that some distant day, they will reappear
to haunt anew the merry-go-round of life.

Spring Eclipse

    Easter having been early this year
    spring gradually unfolds emerald carpet
    over Midwest countryside
    in colors of renewal

while on the small screen
we follow events at half mast
on the spiral path of changing politics

like the president who opened
the Great Wall of China
his shadow now buried
beneath the soil of achievement

construction season unearths
dust clouds that lead
the officeholder over detours
from past to future into history

because the making of peace
is a struggle unequaled
by rooted wars
that fill furrows of time

changing of the guards
at the Walls of Jericho joins
three flags under one God
to part waters of despair

from ashes of apartheid
the Phoenix rises
to unite colors
of one nation's flag

during reports of our soldiers
returned from the Mideast in altered states
we wonder about our stake
in the global connection

    We keep our eye on last year's
    flood swollen river
    that again carries bulging barges
    urged on by smoke stack flags at full mast
    into the next turn

View

The plane drops
from the sky
in front
of the window

remains
suspended
like a toy
for just a moment

then disappears
behind trees
along the river
as if to remind us
life holds
surprises

visions change
according to the room
from which we have
our view

depending
on whether or not
the room has
a window at all

The River

I had only a brief glimpse
of the waters that join this aorta

At Lake Itasca
I stepped across headwaters
as if they were a playful brook

Further south
I saw the atriums of two cities
flank Mark Twain's river
        that awakens in spring
        the pulse of freight yards
        companion of trains
        forested cliffs and caves
        pregnant with cargoed barges
        a river that petrifies in winter's
        mist veiled stories
        in concert with
        ice castle reflections

This river I want to follow
through changing states and
imagination south to the city
        where old river captains
        tell stories of Jean Lafitte
        and raised graveyards
        to the rhythm of jazz
        where every turn of its path
        every tree on its shore
        unfolds stories of the past
        in the shadow and throb
        of sky scraper existence

I want to travel this river
knowing thunder and lightning
past or present
        cannot divide it
        knowing whatever sun consumes
        rain and snow replenish
        and when it rises over its banks
        it reminds me of
nature's untamable power
and when its fish die
        it reminds me
        our attention has strayed

Some day I want to travel this river
from Headwaters to Gulf
from past shadows to sunlight of youth
to connect all the places in between

Runaway

on the flood-swollen
Mississippi
a tree travels south
roots the rudder
leaves the aft sail

    it swiftly passes
    fastened barges

        as if on a mission of joy
        not a log
        or a raft
        but a child
        independent and free

a tugboat moves
to head off the journey
but the tree
sails forward
with that certainty
only energy can assure
power of current
and weight

    steers undiminished
    toward its wherever

the tugboat maneuvers
lines up
with the unwieldy catch
pushes it sidelong
to the shore

    only loaded barges now sway
    to music of metal percussion
    waiting

Spirits of Saint Paul

    Indian mounds rest
    behind wrought iron fences
    face the sky like breasts

It's a one hundred-foot drop
to the swollen river rising
and falling an expectant breath

    by the marker an Indian girl
    smokes a cigarette
    as if to appease the spirits

below the road disappears
sometimes into the river
which washes over what was
giving birth to new vigil

in states south people gather
to sandbag homes and fields
churches and businesses
located on the river plane

    St. Paul's park overflows with sightseers
    men try to place submerged landmarks
    that have weathered other floods
    while their wives look on

    girls on bikes
    "Sprit" contouring their breasts
    pedal their way past them down hill

The river appears peaceful today
barges tethered
beneath clear blue sky

Cathedral bell towers
face Indian mounds
in invocation of watchful spirits

westerly winds brush trees
as if to whisper out of the past
the river gives
the river takes away

Monday Morning

cuddling close
to thoughts of you

    I see you in morning's
    dispersing grey clouds

    in the cluster of bare trees
    on the rise

    and look for you
    on the mist-bedded river

    on the bluffs
    whose flat faced houses
    stare down
    with their windows

    through fog
    and amber lights

    I continue
    into the awakening day past
    yawning stock yards
    and solid business fronts

    to the top of the hill

and enter a block
of concrete and bricks
in fluorescent expanse
filled with a din
of young voices

Unfinished Train Ride

    Distantly, the train rumbles, outrunning the river
    on parallel tracks and ties
    over years of wide-open country,
    playground of hopes and dreams,

back to Berlin where grandmother waited
at the "Bahnsteig" for the train to puff in.
I would sit nestled on father's lap, his throat vibrating
as he spoke. Countryside flew past, tunnels swallowing
the train into darkness that turned on lights
until its release back into daylight.

    New York marked the great shift at our arrival,
    when we observed the world from inside
    the fence of our first language. The journey west
    brought us to obscure nighttime stops and "All aboard!"
    traveling through railroad yards into day,
    past tenements and houses where laundry flew banners,
    past illusive lives sealed in cityscapes,
    until our fence disappeared in open spaces
    of farm-dotted countryside so vast
    a person could vanish forever.
    Indians once raced their horses
    against the iron horse here and against time.

Milwaukee marked the end of the line for us then
and forever, life made new again in this city.
Only the train whistles remained with us
at road intersections and in silence of night.
At home in the entry hall of our house on Murray Avenue,
my brothers created their own world with table-top trains,
trains which inspired father to create tunnels and landscapes
out of cardboard and glue to round out the scene.

      My husband and I took the train from Milwaukee
      to the Twin Cities some years later, starting married life.
      Here we became river and railroad in our parallel existence
      to each other. After the children arrived, I would take them
      to visit their grandparents, at first, by train. This turned into
      an adventure for the toddlers who soon explored the train,
      asking endless questions as miles flew past.

When we would drive through Saint Paul, near the Mississippi,
their father would sometimes stop the car,
while we looked on and the children counted railroad cars,

Soo line and Union Pacific, New York and Los Angeles
box cars, tank cars, and flat cars passing in seemingly
endless progression, like toy trains and animated trains
 in story books at home.

      In my horseshoe existence of home and work,
      I switch roads as readily as languages,
      my car outrunning river and trains,
      first south, passing Burlington Northern,
      Canada to Boston and Maine,
      then west, across the Mississippi,
      then north, past stock yards and truck yards,
      dormant fields on whose fringe
      riverside freight cars labor past river barges
      after exchange of cargo at factories,
      whose billowing smokestacks
      draw the eye into the distance.

On solitary nights, train whistles seep through the dark
and into my dreams with their shrieks, invite
to a wide-open future, to the unexpected, or home.
Like a stow-a-way, I ride aboard right along the Mississippi,
unsure of the next stop, thundering distantly toward light of the next day.

Mississippi River Excursion

We board the boat at Harriet Island in Saint Paul,
near where people look down at the river
and the Mississippi looks up at the city
whose 1st sign reaches up a new kind of church spire.

We came to enjoy dinner from inside our own circle,
looking up at bridges like rainbows set at intervals
whose location and names we try to place
from the perspective of the river that changes all faces,

past Indian mounds, cliffs and caves, roads and railroads,
past skyscrapers and apartments, past power plant
and historic Fort Snelling now hidden behind trees,
past confluence of Minnesota River,
and spilling of Minnehaha Creek into the Mississippi.

But only trees lining the shore are on equal footing
with the River as if guarding its path. Sometimes the river
rises so high, it runs over the city's feet, wanting to be close,
too close. The river washes out trees on the flood plain –
where they fall uprooted.

Tugboats pushing barges, move up and down river
as routinely as tugboat navigators wave
to excursion boats who share the current
in community, making us one for the moment –
spirit of the river.

The river's changing colors reflect its vigil
over comings and goings of creatures and people,
changing landscape and skyline
under clouds and sunshine of passing seasons,
carrying untold stories into the distance.

If you want to know more, just turn to the River,
watchful of the tree line, its turns and current;
navigate your own cruise and return
with the catch of your day – if you can make
the leap across time – if you know where to look.

Echoes of an Ordinary Day

Today I drive across acres of railroad yards
on the Kellogg Boulevard bridge,
connecting segments of my life
in these Twin Cities of bridges.

   I had just returned from Minneapolis
   that very hot day, when 6:00 o'clock
   news reports showed a collapsed bridge,
   steel supports bent like rubber,
   concrete sections broken straight across
   as if they were pieces of gum placed end to end,
   down to and over the water,
   cars, suvs and trucks, like toys,
   randomly resting on broken inclines,
   in cracks of bridge sections,
   except for those visible in the river.
   A truck near a school bus billowed
   smoke and flames like questions of why
   that continuous dousing barely quelled.
   A policeman carried a wounded woman in arms.
   People milled nervously at the perimeter.
   Police cars and ambulances lined up.

Just the Friday before, I dined on an excursion boat
like the one that narrowly missed the collapse,
looking up at bridges from the deck,
majestic bridges and their intricate designs.

   Later that evening, a Minnesota Senator said:
   "Minnesota bridges are not supposed to fall."
   But fall it did, dropping those in traffic
   without regard to age, prenatal status or station in life.

"Someone will be missed tonight," a voice said.
On the screen, the Mississippi eddied
around concrete and cars as if in pain,
dire loss of innocence.

Deficient does not mean the bridge will collapse,
an official surmised from a report.
The dictionary defines "deficient"
as "insufficient," from Latin "to fail."

My daughter called from St. Paul, knowing
I have business in Minneapolis.
My brothers called from Milwaukee and Santa Barbara,
even though it was no one's birthday.

In my sleep scenes of survival
and heroic rescue alternate
with free fall of cars onto broken structure,
of cars plunging into river with their occupants,
some disappearing into its depths,
until I awaken to the safety of the moment.
Thirteen people dead, seventy-nine wounded.

Standing in line at the store the other day,
the woman ahead of me said, smiling:
"At least we are not standing under a bridge."
Yesterday, in Milwaukee at the family celebration,
a friend said Wisconsin's governor now gives
bridge inspection top priority. In Wisconsin Dells
a store clerk noted the bridge into town
carries more and more traffic.

Meanwhile, in Minneapolis the river's water level
is lowered between dams to help navy divers
in rescue and recovery operations.

    Politicians speak of quick rebuilding;
    a lawyer reflects on routes of litigation;
    and the sheriff guards the fence of demarcation
    from intrusion by the curious.
    River captains and barges wait.
    Bridge traffic is officially rerouted.

Today over lunch, we exchange stories
and debate which bridge to avoid,
particularly if it shakes more during rush hour
than prayer or counsel can safeguard.
We consider which bridge we can trust to join parts
of a busy existence into the shape of our daily lives.

Tomorrow we will avoid the topic,
except in passing, and turn in reassurance
to the building of the new bridge.

At the Mississippi South of Saint Paul

      Near where Little Crow and his band once lived,
anchored at the corner of Concord Avenue,
      where Grand Avenue goes up the hill,
a stately structure of four green towers,
      red brick-faced on foundation of gray blocks,
overlooks road, river, and railroad tracks
      like a fortress.

Like the settlers that founded the city,
the old Stockmen's Exchange building
holds its ground over time –
Where cars now park, horses were hitched
in steamboat and horse and buggy days,
while stockyard winds blew.

The building's untimely retirement drew
      pigeons to make upper windows their roost
for years, until one day, dumpsters arrived,
      filling steadily with debris of past years.
Broken, boarded up windows were restored to new vision,
      fresh paint on trim calling attention,
towers presiding in brassy shine once again.

The old edifice now invites, standing reinvented
human voices breathing life into it
as castle hotel, then restaurant, banner flying
of whatever concern can make it –
saved, strength of its construction
in days of vanishing landmarks
and changed stockyard climates.

This landmark, off the endangered species list
      for now, keeps its vigil

over generations of ethnic mix
    populating the community
in shifting winds of time –
    like a parent watching over children.

I will miss passing this old guidepost,
as I no longer travel up the steep hill of public education
to the classroom with a view, in the school
where I filled fifteen years of drawers,
with lessons taught and learned
and days with young voices.

    The pen has reinvented my life,
given wings to my existence,
    crossing the Mississippi River so many times.
I still keep looking for the towers
    when I turn the corner in that direction,
near where eagles have returned,
    where traffic flows in four passageways.

Railroads

    That distant whistle

    pierces fog of dreams
as if summoning to some faraway place
day and night

    "You can't miss them"
the railroad man said
"trains are everywhere in St. Paul"

    and I listen
    time and again
    as if to some secret message

    thoughts stow away
vagrants that sleep
in railroad cars or under bridges
crisscross on tracks too numerous to mention

    freight trains gather
in railroad yards like thoughts
racing the Mississippi carrying barges like stories
by day we watch with fascination
as goods and raw materials of imagination travel
the network of our existence

    unloaded
railroad cars stand in lifeless silence
while workers check engines and repair brakes
at last breathing life into them with new loads
trains are switched and released to new destinations
of our needs and wishes

      the whistle screams
      time and again
      soon daylight will obliterate vision

train whistles
that sweet longing
of compressed days and solitary nights
call us to move on

V
Around the Corner

Roads Between Cities

When we first moved to this area, we found a place in Minneapolis which became home of our newfound independence as young marrieds. After the birth of our children some years later, we moved to Saint Paul to be closer to work. It was not like moving away at all – it seemed like moving from one part of a city to another.

The Mississippi River having given birth to both cities, at foot and head of Saint Anthony Falls, Saint Paul and Minneapolis rise twin giants over surrounding countryside, until they grow together in the middle, their satellites spreading in all directions. Moving between Cities on daily errands, we find roads and streets running into each other, until borders blur, and we lose track of which city we are traveling on continuous streets whose names may or may not change. Many arteries connect suburbs and cities, from Minnetonka to Woodbury and places in between and around and beyond, from freeway and river running through the heart of Twin Cities, from McKnight Road to Lyndale Avenue, Marshall Street to University Avenue, Saint Peter to Nicollet Mall, through skyways and under building tunnels, and on and on.

The Cities vie in competition for our time: What we cannot find in one may exist in the other, somewhere between Indian Mounds Park and Boom Island, Swedenborgian Church and Saint Mary's Basilica, between State Capitol and IDS Tower, between Saint Paul's Court House and Salvation Army, Germanic American Institute and Intermedia Arts, Common Good Books and Amazon Books, Ordway and Orchestra Hall, Winter Carnival and Aquatennial, between Excel Energy Center and Metrodome. We move between landmarks to reach our objective which may be anywhere between 3M and University of

Minnesota, Science Museum and Art Institute, Fitzgerald Theater and Open Book, Minnehaha Falls and Como Park, International Institute and Historical Society, Target Center and Fairview Medical, Amtrak and Greyhound Bus Depot and on. You know in which city you are, because the sun rises over Saint Paul and sets over Minneapolis in the land of perennial smiles, shining over white oak and pine, loon and trout, impatiens and black eyed Susans, lakes and prairie grass, and all the people who live there. Twin Citians know all is well and all manner of things shall be well, in words of Julian of Norwich.

The pyramid of people blurs in the hub of work and events. They say, if you can stand close enough and buy a ticket to the upper life, it is grand. The middle class carries the load; the lower end guards the middle; the homeless wait. A few take without second thought. Sometimes people blend, somehow, that you are not always sure exactly who they are, unless you recognize them or they tell you. We may meet in the daily business of work or charity, in blue northern light of art, music of lakes, stories of river, challenge of sports, diversion of night life, song of the people in their dance of seasons. We move forward speed of industry, sound of technology, test of science, structure of architecture, discourse of religion, community of education, scale of law. Industry and people take the lead, come and go, decline and expand with the times, at railroad yard and in river traffic, at saw mill and flour mill, stockyard and boat yard, brewery and restaurant, department store and dealership, electronics and construction, politics and publishing, cosmetics and medicine, theater and concert hall, office and factory, big industry and small business, at school and at home.

People say this oasis of the Upper Midwest draws residents from small places out west who want to live in a larger metropolis and from large places further east to live in a smaller metropolis and from places beyond for all sorts of reasons. Twin Citians live in the global community of their making. Newcomers and some immigrants blend in quickly; others learn the ropes; and still others cling to the past. They celebrate ethnicity like holidays during the year.

People keep coming. The Cities and surrounding areas keep building. That is why the most notable season of the year is construction here. Because winter is usually cold and snowy, unless it is mild. Spring is short and quickly bursts into green as well as into orange lanes of construction, lasting through the freedom to be outdoors in summer that people long for during long winters and through the splendor of color and mild temperatures of fall. New neighborhoods spring up during this time, like the latest medieval-like city layouts with shops on ground level and apartments upstairs, except for the parking lots and garages that are a part of them. Roads expand and become layered with overpasses and ramps that seem to send us into the clouds. The Cities transform themselves over and over in the blending of times.

Over the years, I lived through many changes in Saint Paul, while I adjusted to life's progression. Minneapolis changed, too, so much so since I first moved there, I had to learn to find my way all over again. Oh, yes, you can get lost in the Twin Cities with the bend of the river, the varying layout of streets – and on-going makeover of buildings and roads. Life can become a tangle of one-way streets, unexpected turns and dead ends, a labyrinth without rules or directions, where effort or landmarks alone are not enough, and you wish you could sprout wings. But instead, you navigate by gut-feel and perseverance, until you reach your destination by grace of God.

In time, you learn to read the transformations like chapters of a city's book. If people leave just enough landmarks, beside the undiminished Minnesota smile and homespun hospitality, you can connect past and present. So you live in one city or its suburb. For what would the suburbs be without the Cities? You work in the other, socialize and play in both, never afraid to rearrange the situation, if it suits the need. Is it any wonder that visitors sometimes call one city by the other's name?

The Twin Cities story is part of my story, now and forever. As the city is made new, so I am made new. The old is gone and lives in memory of old warehouses reinvented. And if I have become more like the Cities, it is because I am Twins. Twin Cities people spring from a strong base, often inscrutable, frequently inquisitive, always creative, and therefore progressive, diverse, amicable, neighborly, a work in progress, navigating waves of change, not always knowing how or where things will come out.

These Twin Cities are two stars to wish upon. You betcha.

At Her Door

delicate stems of
           Smartweed
blue heads of
           Day Flower
flourish

she holds the blossoms
on her open palm
releases them again
priceless jewels

           Angel
tending
           nature's garden

Como Park

 June comes a heat wave this year, sending me
from confinement of house and concrete of city,
to expanse of nature and green of park,
where summer hosts courtship of time.

 The park keeps changing its face
between visits, just as we change with seasons
of our lives. The lake is quiet today, surrounded
by a fence to let ecological plantings restore
its vitality and invite wildlife.

 A flurry of people surrounds the Pavilion,
where I have attended many concerts with friends.
On the other side, the café, where I had lunch
with my brother and nephew a few seasons ago,
is teeming with customers.

 When my children were little and monkey island
still held monkeys, I would pack a picnic lunch
for Sunday outings through park and zoo.

 At the Conservatory, whose entrance now seems
to disappear into expansion, one of my friends
got married among poinsettias some January ago.

 People with children and strollers are streaming
from parking areas into Conservatory and zoo
which have grown together in time.
A wedding has claimed part of the Conservatory

and another the garden across the way, where
the bridal party poses for pictures
between Greek columns to the constant tune

of the merry-go-round,
carried over in warm wind from the zoo.

    Tracing my steps over new concrete footbridge
across the road, I return to Pavilion.
Another wedding is celebrating the day in this space
of concerts and plays. I keep cool with a large scoop
of strawberry ice cream down by the lake, where
young families move about in pontoon boats.

    Today the walking path is deserted
in the day's heat, except for occasional hikers.
A bench invites where two trees lean
in opposite directions, like different lives,

forming a V, my window onto the lake.
I sketch the peaceful scene, because a camera
will not do, and words are not enough
in this marriage of passing times.

Construction Zone

Traveling the accustomed route
life has become
a construction zone
I find myself
on the wrong road
in a city that keeps renewing
did I miss the rust colored sign
midway in existence
from the dead end
of a well traveled marriage
to single life
a throw-back
that carries new momentum

the dream ended
the road here lies torn apart
mounds of earth heave
obscure the old roadbed
old overpasses are down
new ones are not yet passable
the skyline is different
life is different
though the foundation
and I are the same

I don't know the road
on which I suddenly find myself
nor where it will come out
I trace back
to a familiar stretch

Starting over I
determine my own detour

that becomes a new route
it is late and
I accelerate with new purpose
because change is good
watch the needle
on the speedometer
and move toward an uncharted
but beckoning future

Wheels of Fortune

A black Ram diesel truck on raised wheels
roars into the driveway, announcing
my son's arrival. He changes cars as readily

as I do my wardrobe,
Dakota Sport for work,
Charger for errands,
Ram for hauling, and on and on.

> This passion for cars started with matchbox cars
> and toy ramp, giving birth to the boy's dream,
> legacy of inspiration that resulted
> in drawing flaming hot rods in fifth grade,
>
> pictures that now decorate my study wall.
> Soon drawing turned into model building
> that filled shelf, after shelf, after shelf.
>
> From age fifteen he began to refurbish cars
> as if they were a graduation requirement,
> and soon, in spurts of youthful growth, added trucks,
> that he now collects from places local and out-of-state,
>
> provided they are Dodges. In coming of age,
> he gradually moved bookshelf line-up of models,
> from child's play and pastime
>
> to adult's skill of mechanical engineering,
> into the driveway of experimentation,
> then into the workshop of experience,
> and at last to vintage shows of accomplishment.

I get into the world of his truck
like a trapeze artist. The truck looms
a giant, as we head down the road.

He surveys traffic smiling, having arrived at last,
as if standing tall were not enough,
and drives the manhood of his creativity
into the rising sun of the next model Jeep.

Starting Out

   Having looked for over two months, we found
a place on Russell Avenue at the end of the block
when we first came to live in Minneapolis
shortly after we were married.

   Today I find the double bungalow almost as if
I had just returned from an errand, nestling
between trees and shrubs on top of the hill.
It sports the same fresh white coat of paint,
the same black window frames and shutters
as when we first called it home.

The same two sets of steps lead up the steep hillside
from the sidewalk, each with a banister, the original
cast iron one at the top, a new wooden one leading up
from below, along steps that want to shift into a spiral
that belies the like-new appearance of the house.

I used to take the bus at the corner of Broadway
to work or downtown. One day, on my way home,
a little boy playing in front of his house looked up
to me and said: "I wish you were my mommy."

It renewed my wish to have children of my own.
They were soon to be born here, first the daughter,
then the son, only fourteen months apart. The babysitter
would say they were like uneven twins –
what you do for one you have to do for the other.

A new mom, the adventure of parenting began
with my daughter. And one snowy winter day,
without transportation and my husband out of town,
I rushed on foot, with the newborn wrapped in blankets,

to the doctor on Broadway Avenue. He pronounced
the baby well and doing fine.

When my son was born, my mother came to care
for my daughter and my peace of mind. I gave her
a red leather purse afterwards to hold our mother-
daughter bond. Parenting quickly expanded
but this time, I was better prepared.

On pleasant days, I took the babies for walks
around the block in the double stroller,
while neighborhood dogs gathered around us.

Sitting on steps at side entrance of the house,
I wrote long letters about the children to my parents,
first smile, first words, first steps, first scrape
and read Doctor Spock, whose advice, except
for the health issues, seemed incredible to me.

This house that rooted our lives in the Twin Cities
appears almost as if I never left, after so many years,
as if all I have to do is go inside
and get the kids up from their naps.

At the Arboretum
        for Lee and Jerry

My friends and I rest on the bench
    overlooking the pond
hand-made
    like a Monet
renewable
    like our friendship

muddy emerald water
    mirrors yellow flowers
and birch trees in shade
    of late August sunshine
along life's visitor path

we look for that
    which we don't know
or have lost
    children reading clouds

and find the old familiar
    in this Noah's Ark
of gardens
    reconnecting earth and sky

making existence new again
    we become gardeners
in reflection of the Father
    root and stem
of our creation

A Taste of Minnesota

St. Paul built onto wooded bluffs
of the Mississippi River
lies lulled in clouds
the pulsing river at its feet
steadfast

layers of a social order
of people converge
a Fourth of July parade
at the foot of the capitol
the cultural mix
streams past roses
to taste hot dogs and corn on the cob
staples of their celebration
pulsing

My daughter and I drift
past vendors and food booths
through 224 years of independence
at the pinnacle of a new age
to revisit the bygone and move forward
with ice cream cones
talk and laughter of our freedom
carrying the water of our friendship
we try on sun dresses
that tie the mother-daughter bond
anew

Happy Birthday America
we'll watch the fireworks
of expansion and growth
the right to seek refuge
in wide open spaces

to come and go in a crowd
or to retreat
behind the third story club window
near the Mississippi River bluff
in celebration of all Fourth of Julys
a country's tradition
the family's tradition

rhythm
set to music
of a warm summer night
the river in darkness below
pulsing
in continuity

The Man with the Rose

The grey-haired man
in powder blue jacket
carries a pink rose with baby's breath
in a white bud vase.
He strolls among
"Sommerfest" plaza crowd
as though looking
for a shrine
on which to place the rose,
drawing eyes
that want to know.

"He is looking for his blind date.
I would die for a rose!"
a woman in pink dress says.
She follows his movements
moving closer
to the tumbleweed
of her fantasy.
She turns to her friend:
"Go, talk to him!"
He replies with a wink:
"Oh, no, he may think
I am the date."

Saturating warm evening air
with discussion of business ventures,
we watch Ukranian dancers,
aware only
of a celebrity's shadow
crossing the plaza,
as we follow
through a gray screen
in the corner of an eye
the torch of an untold story -
the man with the rose.

Company

Dressed in worn clothes,
hair frayed
below wool caps,
an old man and an old woman
sit in the entry
of a house visiting
next door to paradise.

They chat
sharing a smoke
in late afternoon
brightened
by light snow.

They do not notice
the cold
that sends shoppers
hurriedly past
into Seward's store.

They sit a long time,
smiling uneven smiles,
rubbing shoulders,
comfortable,
at home with each other
on the street
of forlorn hope.

First and Third Saturdays

We meet at Seward's Café this summer
to keep the round open
in the poet's booth where we enjoy
refreshment and conversation between regulars

> troubadour laureate
> who knows true iambs and villanelles
> to become what he perceives

> ethereal spirit
> who stretches between earth and sky
> to touch

> distant observer
> who presents a slice of life
> each time

> lamp in father's hand
> who chooses the microscopic view
> and the vehicle

> veteran lover
> whose golden arms embrace
> and hold

> caller
> whose words stir refrain as well as
> any other voice in the group

And the drop-ins
listen and clarify

and pass the coffee

Among members lost in limbo
of another state are those who surface
from the depths of their absence

please pass the coffee

One presiding on the mountain
of his Olympus

Another voyageur on the rivers
of salmon fishing

Another fisherman tackling line in Montana
and poetry in Minnesota

Another striding through ancient gardens
of Babylon

Still another at the green light
of youthful imagination

We pass the coffee one more time

The language is natural as the food
the responses pure as mineral water

Those who hang in there for dessert
pass the cookies with talk of letting
wolf or chickadee out of the jacket

We study chameleon
challenge tiger
on occasion retreat into
our own turtle existence
discuss Rilke and Yeats
Wordsworth and Masters
Sarton and St. Vincent Millay

In shadow of Jung and Bly
and other adventurers
we depart to travel
Mississippi and St. Croix
rivers of our lives
to explore each our own
Boundary Waters

Tribute to Richard Gisselquist

We met at the Loft
on Franklin Avenue in Minneapolis
on first and third Saturdays
of the month, beginning
in the late 1980s, until 1994
when the Open Group sealed
their poetry in the anthology
that prepared us for Stage Two
of our Poetic Lives.

When Richard read,
he did not waste words
but hammered them out
with the precision of an engineer,
economy of a word smith,
mystery and imagination of an artist.

After the meetings,
his pretty young wife would be waiting
at the restaurant,
and while everyone filed in singly,
we enjoyed their unity.

When Richard joined Chaparral Poets
later on, he read
the poetry of contestants
not so much with the query of judge
as the grace of saint.

Richard's life is
like an unfinished book,
though the pages have been written.

We will miss him
for the song
of his carefully crafted words,
the cadences of his humor
but most of all,
we will miss him
for the halting smile
that punctuated
the reading of his poems.

Chance Meeting

He stepped into
the lighted doorway
of my vision and
we met across
the round table

of our new day
we talked more
than we danced

then in transition's hallway
he waited with me
for a friend
till time to go

a familiar
softness behind
fine-rimmed glasses
stirred a wanting to know
more of him

Ballroom Extravaganza at the Dance Shoppe

Dancing
releases the soul
into the body's movements
at the United Nations of ballroom instruction
where every dance represents a different passion
in languages ranging
from swing to tango to waltz
in various ballrooms of lessons
      Anyone can learn

I rediscover the old dances
that have reappeared
with new moves and rules
where steps change the dance
but the swing stays the same
      for what makes a dance

At last I remember
to push out collar bone
head in position
balance in the middle
feet finding their way
knees a bit springy
for that Fred Astaire movement
      that makes a dancer

twinkles and turns
spins and grape vines
take me
from one lesson
to another
until steps become rhythm to the music
and to each partner's style
      in this conversation of body language

rock step   one and two
"You're standing too straight"
      a swing partner says

one   two   three
"You are too good at this"
      a waltz partner says

one   two   one two three
"Just keep taking lessons"
      a cha cha partner says

on the crowded ballroom floor
of life's hometown lessons
I often wonder
if I will ever
get it right
      what makes a dance partner
        rock step

Dance Partner

    Swing dancing is
free will touching hands
past brought to present
    rock   rock   rock

    pulling close
touching fingers to the rhythm
turn and twirl as if to
    flirt   flirt   flirt

    in the untwining
of mind and body
the heart rocks to the
    beat   beat   beat

    and the spirit flying
out arms length
unfurls the shadows
    step   step   step

    'round the lyrics
"pretty woman" and each other
to the "hound dog"
    back   back   back

    through the language
of body swaying to the music
free at last
    clap   clap   clap

Twin City Valentine

     So often we drove
Twin Cities streets
unfamiliar to me

streets that continue
between cities
as if they were one

     I look for the place
on the Minneapolis side
of University Avenue changing
from two way to one way and two way again
to deliver
the Valentine's Day reading
he seeded into my head

I wind my way
in shadow of past rides
as his stories revisit
times when he revealed
his life to me until
it seemed part of my own
until he went south to live

     I see now where
these streets continue
and where
they travel one way only

At Saint Paul City Hall

    In the mayor's office
people and art blend today
    into everyday business of the city
poets and artists invited
    the mayor shaking hands

    On the wall
aerial photograph of Saint Paul's
    technological age lets the eye trace
the city's center that rose
    out of yesterday's tired old buildings
to today's transformed eye-lifting skyline
    around which arteries of road converge
like a burst of sun rays

    From the mayor's window
you can watch city streets
    alive with people and traffic
glimpse the Mississippi
    just beyond Kellogg Boulevard
Past Salvation Army kettle of lights
    where further south and east
the mayor connected
    Shepherd and Warner Roads
for us to travel as one
    from yesterday to tomorrow

    In waning days of his office
we connect politics and poetry
    over cookies and conversation
in an exhibit celebrating
    art and family housing

coming from different directions
    we all travel the distance today
of one mind
    where present is rotating platform
and future issues from past monuments
    each an eye on the vibrant city

Ice Palace Legend

      Ice palaces come and go
in St. Paul. They warm us away
from mid-winter blues. Endless
as headlights lining street, people
await the vision time and again.

Cranes of Paul Buyan-like arms
raise ice blocks from a Minnesota lake
this year. Timeless as wishes,
they are placed one by one
to create the fortress of imaginings
in this marriage of fantasy and reality.

      Rainbow lights undulate through towers,
draw us into magic incantation of computer age
in the land of northern lights,
in this season of frozen river and lakes,
where Winter Carnival royalties reign
and north winds rule during days of crystal sun
and nights of lighted trees
in courtyard of hockey tournaments,
near arena of ice shows,
not far from honor guard of ice sculptures,
in ritual of torchlight parades
that inspire their own victory dance
for ever-present crowds.

      But winter's reverie cannot be left
to the great melt. The castle bears
careful dismantling before the fateful hour,
return to its source the dream
that will transform and reappear
next generation of castles
who knows when and where.

      Ice palaces hold moments
longer than seasons.

At the Grocery Store

After words of praise and reminiscence
at the funeral of a friend's father,
I stop at the grocery store

and find it still quiet
in early afternoon,
before arrival of rush hour crowd.

Rounding the aisle for Ivory snow,
I suddenly find myself crossing back
to the land of the active.

Two white-haired ladies exchange greetings
so heartily and loudly,
I am tempted to join them for a party.

Rounding the next corner looking
for paper towels,
I find them still in lively conversation.

The taller of the two, with her distinct accent,
insists: "Then you must say something.
You must tell them how you feel!"

The other woman, bent with weight of years,
responds: "Oh no, I won't say anything.
I don't want to make waves."

As I head for the check-out, I wonder why
mopping up spills with paper towels
only looks fun in commercials.

As I walk to the car, I wonder why
the silence of living haunts more
than the reminiscence on death.

What's for Dinner?

What's for dinner at the Germanic-American Institute
on Saint Paul's Summit Avenue invites through the bright
front door of the present or the dim corridor of the past, glimpses

in a harbor of things German. On member night, visitors,
members, and guests alike are seated around the table
family style for a communion of cultural perspectives,

without regard to ethnicity or place of origin. The meal
prepared from German recipes with American ingredients,
like Schnitzel mit Spaetzle, followed with Kuchen,

would do any restaurant proud. People arrive
in a confluence of different currents of time,
place, and background. They range from those

whose forebears settled the land to those
who immigrated consequence of twentieth-century
events and wars to those whose jobs or vacations bring them.

They share views in octaves of round-table songs
where for some history abounds in parts
of American landscapes and for some, the clock stopped

at their time of arrival in the new world. Others are
as at home in America as in the German-speaking
countries they frequent, while still others volley

between cultures, and the rest blend their diverse
encounters into the all-American, until they lose track
which is which, trying to decide between platforms

of Democrats and Republicans for the good
of the country that is their home, wishing more countries
had the benefit of the Civil Rights Movement

to help them move forward as surely as they know
"Lederhosen" is the American stereotype for German,
just as the cowboy hat is for American.

They hold meetings following Roberts Rules of Order,
because the Germanic-American Institute is a showcase
of living culture, past and present mixing into a new

version. Sometimes they rewrite old world traditions to conform
to present-day American standards, politically correct,
leaving the newcomer to ponder. Still, the two worlds exist

side-by-side, sometimes like planets, but more like siblings,
like their languages of English and German, of one family
that connects and reconnects at the round table of friendship.

The Spectator

In the dream, bicycle races were on.
Standing at the corner of Kellogg
and John Ireland Boulevards, I watched with awe
as cyclists pedaled uphill, past St. Paul Cathedral
and down Summit Avenue.

A young man stood on the far side of the street
reading aloud names of participants.
I wanted to join the race.

> When I was a kid, I never owned a bike,
> and I had not sat on one since that disastrous
> encounter with a tree in early days of my marriage,
> when I tried to learn to ride one.

In the dream, I thought surely, if they could ride
so well, at least I could try, and if disaster struck again –
But perhaps I could just make it to the finish line
on my own time –

> There are so many things I never got to do –
> because of bad times or being female,
> or living in too many different places,
> or having too many responsibilities,
> busy standing on the sidelines, cheering –

But then I wondered what it really was
that held me back lately. Times had changed.
Had I not evolved with the times, teaching
the young by the new rules? Perhaps it seemed
easier to retreat to the house and garden
of a familiar world than face the unknown.

Yet I wanted to join the people out there, balance
with pen and paper in the marathon of life,
move forward, starting at the Boulevard of Love,
breathing up the steep hill of Reflection
to the Avenue of Truth, energy of words,
over distance of language –
to the finish line of Community.

The Field Across the Street

    For years I watched corn grow tall
where crows and geese gathered in the fall,
and wind blew
through divide of well-rooted trees
    in fields across the street.

    Rarely did I ever see
the farmer till the land that was
woods and prairie when Indians lived there,
    saw it hushed in darkness every night.

    One day the realtor said
smiling across dinner table:
"Let's grow houses instead of corn"
    in these surrounding fields.

    Houses grew and condominiums,
banks and filling stations,
malls and shops and restaurants and more.
In what once were fields across the street,
    parking lots now fill with cars.

    Concrete and brick buildings,
in place of corn, blend into a cloudy sky today –
cycle of people leaving the country,
looking for work in the city,
moving to suburb looking for space,
then sprawling beyond as if to reclaim land
grandparents once owned –
    in fields across the street.

    Geese gather on landscaped green,
where workers plant seedling trees
near man-made ponds.
A wall of lighted signs glares back all night
    from the parking lot across the street.

> Only one field still remains,
> a remnant, awaiting its fate, divided
> by windbreaker trees facing the setting sun,
> where I rarely see the farmer till the land,
> hushed in darkness every night.

As the Blue Heron Flies

     above trees
the wide-eyed moon

     faces
the golden-haloed sun

     slipping
behind rooftops

     pulling night
sky between them

In the Dark

We talk
        we dance
sometimes we drive for hours
        to find
that certain unknown place
        to talk
        and dance
        some more

sometimes we lose
        our way
fill spaces between stars
        with conversation

for in the seeking
        we enjoy
        the passage
        and discover
the unexpected

The Author

Evelyn Klein's poetry and prose combine observation and memoir in her examination of human nature in the ever-present quest for establishing community in a time of transience. The community becomes a kind of extended family in *Once upon a Neighborhood*, as it does for so many people in this country today. Placed in a frame of prose against a backdrop of scenic drawings, her poetry style varies with the subject matter.

Evelyn D. Klein is a freelance writer/teacher/artist. At intervals, she has also served as editor and writing judge. A prize-winning poet, Klein's work has appeared in numerous anthologies, journals, newspapers, and other publications. Most recently, her article "Breaking Through the Wall of Resistance" appeared in A View from the Loft. She edited and published the multicultural anthology, *Stage Two: Poetic Lives* (illustrated by her father, Wolfgang Klein). Her prize-winning poem, "A Place Called Home" was chosen in 2004 by the Family Housing Fund for inclusion in the "Home Sweet Home Again" exhibit of art and poetry still touring the Twin Cities area, along with the recently added poem "The Empty House." (Two other poems, excerpts of From Here Across the Bridge, were selected by the Family Housing Fund for their Annual Report Calendars.) In 2006 she published the poetry memoir, From Here Across the Bridge, including art from her father, Wolfgang Klein, with Nodin Press.

Klein went to high school in Milwaukee, Wisconsin, and earned her bachelor of science in Secondary Education at the University of Wisconsin Milwaukee and her master of science degree in the Teaching of English at the University of Wisconsin-River Falls. She taught language arts and German in the public schools in Wisconsin and Minnesota for many years. During that time, she led a poetry group at the Loft Literary Center in Minneapolis for seven years and currently teaches writing there and at other venues.

NORMANDALE COMMUNITY COLLEGE
LIBRARY
9700 FRANCE AVENUE SOUTH
BLOOMINGTON, MN 55431-4399